I0087429

A CourseGuide for

Church History

Volume Two

John D. Woodbridge
Frank A. James III

ZONDERVAN
ACADEMIC

ZONDERVAN ACADEMIC

A CourseGuide for Church History, Volume Two:
From Pre-Reformation to the Present Day

Copyright © 2019 by Zondervan

ISBN 978-0-310-11020-0 (softcover)

Requests for information should be addressed to:
Zondervan, *3900 Sparks Dr. SE, Grand Rapids, Michigan 49546*

Printed in the United States of America

CONTENTS

Introduction 5

1. European Christianity in an Age of Adversity,
   Renaissance, and Discovery (1300–1500) 7

2. The Renaissance and the Christian Faith 10

3. Luther's Reformation 13

4. The Swiss Reformations 16

5. Radicals and Rome 19

6. Reformations in England 22

7. Refining the Reformation 25

8. Christianity in an Age of Fear, Crisis, and Exploration
   (17th Century) 28

9. Christianity and the Question of Authority
   (17th Century) 31

10. Christianity under Duress 34

11. Christianity in the Age of Lights (1) 37

12. Christianity in the Age of Lights (2) 40

13. Christianity in the Age of Lights (3) 43

14. Christianity in an Age of Revolutions (1770–1848) 46

15. Adjusting to Modernization and Secularism 49

16. Nineteenth-Century Christianity in the British Isles 52

17. The Christian Churches on the European Continent
    (1814–1914) 55

18. Global Christianity 58

19. Modern Theological Trajectories 61

20. Catholicism and Orthodoxy 64

21. Contemporary American Evangelicalism 67

22. Christianity and Islam 70

Introduction

Welcome to *A CourseGuide for Church History, Volume Two: From Pre-Reformation to the Present Day*. These guides were created for formal and informal students alike who want to engage deeper in biblical, theological, or ministry studies. We hope this guide will provide an opportunity for you to grow not only in your understanding, but also in your faith.

How to Use this Guide

This guide is meant to be used in conjunction with the book *Church History, Volume Two: From Pre-Reformation to the Present Day* and its corresponding videos, *Church History, Volume Two Video Lectures* After you have read each chapter in the book and watched the accompanying video lesson, the materials in this guide will help you review and assess what you have learned. Application-oriented questions are included as well.

Each CourseGuide has been individually designed to best equip you in your studies, but in general, you can expect the following components. Most CourseGuides begin every chapter with a "You Should Know" section, which highlights key terminology, people, and facts to remember. This section serves as a helpful summary for directing your studies. Reflection questions, typically two to three per chapter, prompt you to summarize key points you've learned. Discussion questions invite you to an even deeper level of engagement. Finally, most chapters will end with a short quiz to test your retention. You can find the answer key to each quiz at the bottom of the page following it.

For Further Study

CourseGuides accompany books and videos from some of the world's top biblical and theological scholars. They may be used independently, or in small groups or classrooms, offering quality instruction to equip students for academic and ministry pursuits. If you would like to engage in further study with Zondervan's CourseGuides, the full lineup may be viewed online. After completing your studies with *A CourseGuide for Church History, Volume Two: From Pre-Reformation to the Present Day*, we recommend moving on to *A CourseGuide for Introduction to Biblical Interpretation, A CourseGuide for How to Read the Bible for All Its Worth*, and *A CourseGuide for Know How We Got Our Bible*.

CHAPTER 1

European Christianity in an Age of Adversity, Renaissance, and Discovery (1300–1500)

You Should Know

- Due to the complexities of rapid social, political, and religious change, the experience of European Christians in the late Middle Ages (c. 1300–1500) defies easy generalizations.

- The "Great Schism" began with the election of two popes in 1378.

- Although it overcame scandal and internal dissent to reassert its claim as supreme authority over a unified Christendom on the eve of the Protestant Reformation, in reality the papacy lost much of its former influence over increasingly powerful European rulers.

- The Conciliar Movement arose as a response to the schism, claiming that church power is vested in the entire "congregation of the faithful" and should be exercised through councils. The initial result was not promising.

- The Council of Constance tried to reform the church by providing for the regular holding of councils.

- The council issued the decree *Frequens* (1417) that called for regular councils as a defense against heresy and corruption.

- The decades following the Council of Constance saw the rise of "Renaissance Popes," who sought to reestablish papal power.

- A Line of Demarcation was drawn by Pope Alexander VI in 1493 to separate the exploration efforts of Spain and Portugal.

- By the end of the fifteenth century, the papacy had survived tumultuous decades of adversity, renaissance, and discovery to maintain its visible role as supreme head of a unified Christendom. At the same time, the shift in European politics toward strong regional monarchs was a check on papal power.

Reflection Questions

1. Why might one call the fifteenth century an "Age of Adversity?" In what ways did Europeans in the late Middle Ages attempt to explain the difficulties they faced daily?

2. How was nationalism expressed in the late Middle Ages? Why was this a threat to the old ideal of a unified "Christendom"?

3. Explain the relationship between art and the papacy in the era of "Renaissance Popes."

Discussion Question

1. Describe the three goals the Council of Constance (1414–18) set out to accomplish. How do all three of these goals relate to questions about the nature of authority in the church?

Quiz

1. (T/F) Late medieval Europeans understood the devastation resulting from war, disease, and natural disasters to be random occurrences.

2. (T/F) By some estimates, Europe's population fell by two-thirds between 1300 and 1450.

3. (T/F) Papal power in the fourteenth century was strengthened by the rise of strong regional monarchs and princes.

4. (T/F) Catherine of Siena played an important role in ending the "Babylonian Captivity of the Church."

5. (T/F) The poet Petrarch had a positive view of the papacy.

6. (T/F) The Conciliar Movement sought to end conflicts between European monarchs by calling for political assemblies.

7. (T/F) The Ottoman conquest of Constantinople in 1453 was celebrated by the pope and other leaders of the Catholic Church.

8. "The Babylonian Captivity of the Church" refers to:

   a) The capture of Pope Benedict VIII by supporters of Philip IV in 1303
   b) The relocation of the papacy in Avignon from 1309–1377
   c) A poem about Israel composed by the poet and humanist Petrarch
   d) None of the above

9. Which of the following is associated with attempts to restore the artistic and architectural splendor of Rome in the late fifteenth and early sixteenth centuries?

   a) The "Renaissance Popes"
   b) Niccolò Machiavelli
   c) Baselites
   d) The Council of Pisa

10. John Hus was:

    a) Chancellor of the University of Prague
    b) A follower of the ideas of the Englishman John Wycliffe
    c) Condemned as a heretic in 1415 by the Council of Constance
    d) All of the above

CHAPTER 2

The Renaissance and the Christian Faith

You Should Know

- Renaissance humanism, with its appreciation for the knowledge and culture of antiquity, emerged within a culture deeply rooted in a long Christian tradition.

- Although often at odds with the philosophical approach of scholasticism, Christian humanists generally applied humanistic learning and methods to support, not to undermine, the Christian faith.

- The humanist *ad fontes* approach to studying ancient texts from the earliest manuscripts created an interest across Europe in the Bible's original languages.

- A combination of humanistic learning and biblical studies led to early calls within the church for reform according to Scripture that would influence the beliefs of many Protestant leaders.

- Some adherents of "Christian humanism" emphasized the Bible's authority and the imitation of Christ's life and teachings. Other forms of Christian humanism saw Catholic scholars applying humanistic methods to studying the church fathers and Scripture.

- "Renaissance": derived from a French word that means to be "reborn"

- Renaissance humanism: a movement often associated with a high view of human ability and a celebration of the achievements of ancient pagan culture

- Johannes Gutenberg: a German publisher known for introducing moveable type and the printing press

- Desiderius Erasmus: Although he did not break from the Catholic Church, he pursued interests in humanistic and biblical studies that led him toward "reforming" concerns.

Reflection Questions

1. In what ways was humanistic education different from the scholastic approaches more common at the beginning of the Renaissance? How did each define an educated person?

2. Why were humanists so interested in getting back to the original sources of the texts they studied? What impact did this have on Christian approaches to studying the Bible?

3. Discuss developments in European society during the Renaissance that might have contributed to the development and spread of Reformation ideas.

Discussion Question

1. Explain the central concerns of Renaissance "humanism" and whether it was intrinsically hostile to Christianity. Was it possible to be a Christian humanist? Explain and support your answer.

Quiz

1. (T/F) There is general agreement among scholars to refer to the period between 1300 and 1700 as an era of European "Renaissance."

2. (T/F) Historical evidence proves that Renaissance humanism was a rejection of Christian faith and morals.

3. (T/F) Fourteenth-century Italian thinkers such as Petrarch and Boccacio thought of their own time as a period of cultural rebirth after centuries of cultural darkness.

4. (T/F) Coluccio Salutati argued that studying the liberal arts could benefit the church.

5. (T/F) Girolamo Savonarola was an ardent supporter of the Renaissance in Florence.

6. (T/F) "Christian Hebraism" took an interest in Hebrew language and Jewish history.

7. (T/F) Women enjoyed relative equality with men during the Renaissance era.

8. *Ad fontes* refers to the humanist concern to find and study what manuscript sources of both pagan and Christian literature?
   a) Revised
   b) Original
   c) Ancient
   d) Modern

9. Petrarch criticized the scholastic theologians for:
   a) Failing to appreciate the cultural riches of the "Middle Ages"
   b) Failing to use philosophy to promote the art of living well
   c) Failing to raise and examine enough difficult questions
   d) All of the above

10. Christian humanists:
    a) Wanted to base their faith on linguistic study of Scripture
    b) Appreciated the abstract philosophical methods of Scholastic theologians
    c) Sought to undermine Christian teaching with human-centered thinking
    d) None of the above

CHAPTER 3

Luther's Reformation
A Conscience Unbound

You Should Know

- Martin Luther did not initially intend to break from the Catholic Church when he posted his *Ninety-Five Theses* in 1517 to begin a debate over the practice of selling indulgences.

- Luther's distinctive theology, including his doctrine of justification by faith alone, developed over time and his opposition to Rome hardened as he was provoked by the Catholic Church and refused to recant what he believed to be the Bible's clear teaching.

- While the Reformation centered on theological convictions, it also involved cultural, socioeconomic, and political factors that enabled Luther's ideas to spread, take hold, and divide Europe as they did in the sixteenth century.

- Through his reading of Scripture as well as Augustine's theology, Luther became convinced over time that justification was not by works, but by faith alone.

- The presenting issue that unleashed the Reformation was the Catholic Church's campaign to raise money through the sale of indulgences.

- The belief that the Pope had power to dispense merit for removing the temporal punishments of sin stood behind the practice of selling indulgences.

- One of Luther's major accomplishments during his year in hiding at the Wartburg Castle was his influential translation of the New Testament into German.

- The Augsburg Confession: the statement of Protestant beliefs drafted by Melanchthon in 1530 and refuted by Catholic theologians without further debate

Reflection Questions

1. Was a decisive break with Rome necessary? Discuss whether Luther's concerns could have been addressed from within the Catholic Church.

2. Describe the theological basis for the sale of indulgences and the ways in which this practice could have been abused.

3. In what sense was the Reformation about the question of proper authority? Give examples from Luther's life and writings to support your answer.

Discussion Question

1. Discuss the difference between reading "the righteousness of God" in Romans 1:17 as an attribute of God versus interpreting this phrase to mean the righteousness of Christ with which God clothes sinners. Does justification by faith alone mean a disregard for good works? Why or why not?

Quiz

1. (T/F) Elector Frederick the Wise of Saxony is credited with saving Luther's life.

2. (T/F) Luther supported the Peasants' Revolt as an expression of Christian freedom.

3. (T/F) The Peace of Augsburg (1555) was a victory for religious toleration.

4. (T/F) The Reformation shifted criteria for a good marriage toward mutual affection.

5. (T/F) Support for the Reformation was sometimes a matter of political strategy.

6. The statement of Protestant beliefs drafted by Melanchthon in 1530 and refuted by Catholic theologians was called:

   a) The Peace of Augsburg
   b) The Augsburg Confession
   c) The Ninety-Five Theses
   d) The Wartburg Confession

7. The sacrament of penance defined by the Fourth Lateran Council (1215) involves which of the following?

   a) Contrition
   b) Confession
   c) Absolution
   d) All of the above

8. Protestants were unified in their rejection of:

   a) Transubstantiation
   b) Infant baptism
   c) Marriage for priests
   d) None of the above

9. Which of the following groups claimed to carry on Luther's theological legacy?

   a) Philippists
   b) Gnesio-Lutherans
   c) Both A & B
   d) None of the above

10. "Evangelical" in the sixteenth century was another word for:

   a) Protestant
   b) The Pope
   c) Lawyer
   d) Saint

ANSWER KEY

1. T, 2. F, 3. F, 4. T, 5. T, 6. B, 7. D, 8. A, 9. C, 10. A

CHAPTER 4

The Swiss Reformations

The Maturation of International Calvinism (16th Century)

You Should Know

- The Reformation's establishment in sixteenth-century Switzerland was influenced by the region's unique political situation as a confederation of autonomous "cantons," as well as by Geneva's history as an independent city with close ties to the Swiss Confederation.

- Zwingli's leadership in Zürich embraced a "magisterial reformation" that helped establish Protestantism in the Swiss territories and was a key precursor to the Reformed tradition.

- Calvin's leadership in Geneva contributed in the consolidation and expansion of the Reformed branch of Protestantism, of which Calvin himself emerged as an important theological source among several early leaders including Bucer, Bullinger, and Vermigli.

- In the sixteenth century, foreign rulers often enlisted the Swiss as mercenaries.

- The Marburg Colloquy failed because of different views concerning the nature of Christ's presence in the Eucharist.

- Calvin was banished from Geneva in 1538 and spent three years in Strasbourg.

- Under Calvin's leadership, Geneva became an important center for training and sending missionaries in the sixteenth century.

- Their opponents viewed the Anabaptist movement's rejection of infant baptism as both religious heresy and political treason.

Reflection Questions

1. Describe the differences between Luther and Zwingli at the Marburg Colloquy. How would you characterize Calvin's position on the Lord's Supper in relation to theirs?

2. In what ways did Zwingli both encourage and oppose the development of Anabaptism?

3. In what ways were Zwingli and Calvin similar to Luther? How were they different?

Discussion Question

1. Is it accurate to call Calvin the "father of the Reformed faith"? Explain and support your answer. Identify two popular misconceptions about Calvin's theology and address these with examples from his writings and ministry in Geneva.

Quiz

1. The 1522 "Sausage Affair" in Zürich was primarily about:
   a) The rejection of rules not found in Scripture
   b) The importance of sausage-making to the city's economy
   c) Zwingli's near-death experience ministering to plague victims
   d) None of the above

2. Heinrich Bullinger:
   a) Succeeded Luther as leader of the reform in Wittenberg
   b) Wrote the influential Second Helvetic Confession
   c) Helped unite the Zwinglian and Anabaptist branches of the Reformation
   d) All of the above

3. Which of the following is associated with Calvin's years in Strasbourg (1538–41)?

    a) Pastoring the French refugee congregation

    b) Writing his commentary on the biblical book of Romans

    c) Friendship with Martin Bucer and development of Calvin's theology

    d) All of the above

4. Calvin's *Institutes of the Christian Religion* exhibits the theological influence of:

    a) Karl Barth

    b) Augustine

    c) John Knox

    d) Konrad Grebel

5. (T/F) The city of Geneva was a member of the Swiss Confederation.

6. (T/F) John Calvin converted to Protestantism through the efforts of Guillaume Farel.

7. (T/F) Calvin enjoyed strong support in Geneva from the start of his ministry there.

8. (T/F) His friendship with Martin Bucer had a deep influence on Calvin's theology.

9. (T/F) Geneva's church was restructured upon Calvin's return to that city in 1541.

10. (T/F) Michael Servetus tirelessly defended the orthodox doctrine of the Trinity.

CHAPTER 5

Radicals and Rome

Responses to the Magisterial Reformation (16th Century)

You Should Know

- The widespread spiritual and social discontent that buttressed Luther's reformation shows itself in the almost immediate emergence of movements calling for deeper religious change than Luther intended, even using Luther's theology to justify violent uprisings.

- While diverse in its various strains and difficult to categorize, the Anabaptist movement seems to have originated in the Swiss Brethren's stress on adult rebaptism in Zürich.

- The Catholic Counter-Reformation addressed the necessity of moral renewal within the church while also reaffirming traditional Catholic doctrine over against Protestant beliefs.

- The Anabaptist community established by Jacob Hutter in Moravia was known for its complete sharing of wealth.

- In 1532 radicals seized and violently established an apocalyptic "kingdom" in the city of Münster.

- Socinianism: a movement committed to measuring doctrine according to the standard of reason

- The *zelanti*: a faction in the Catholic Church that sought reform through suppression of the Protestants and reasserting traditional Catholic teachings

Reflection Questions

1. Why did both Protestants and Catholics consider Anabaptists and Radicals a threat?

2. Explain differences between Anabaptists, magisterial reformers (Protestants), and Catholics in terms of their views of authority. Give examples to support your answer.

3. Describe the goals, specific strategies, and outcome of the Catholic Counter-Reformation.

Discussion Question

1. Discuss the challenges of using the term "Anabaptist" to define a sixteenth-century reform movement. Compare and contrast three different Anabaptist groups. What made each one unique? In what sense can we refer to them all as "Anabaptists"?

Quiz

1. (T/F) Pacifism was a commitment characteristic of many main-stream Anabaptists.

2. (T/F) The apocalyptic orientation of Melchiorite theology was intrinsically violent.

3. (T/F) Ignatius of Loyola belonged to the Catholic Church's moderate *spirituali* faction.

4. (T/F) The Index of Prohibited Books included translations of the Bible.

5. (T/F) Thomas Aquinas was declared a heretic by the Council of Trent.

6. (T/F) Ignatius of Loyola taught his followers absolute obedience to the pope.

7. Michael Sattler was:

    a) The primary author of the *Schleitheim Articles* (1527)
    b) Tortured and burned at the stake
    c) Influenced by the ideas of the Swiss Brethren
    d) All of the above

8. Which of the following was a branch of sixteenth-century Anabaptism?

    a) Mennonites
    b) Hittites
    c) Philippists
    d) Jesuits

9. Which of the following was NOT addressed by the Council of Trent?

    a) Renewing devotional practices
    b) Transubstantiation
    c) Polygamy
    d) Scripture and tradition

10. The Peace of Westphalia (1648) did which of the following?

    a) Granted individual rulers the right to determine their territory's religion
    b) Ended conflicts between Christians and the Ottoman Empire
    c) Established the kingdom of Münster
    d) None of the above

ANSWER KEY
1. T, 2. F, 3. F, 4. T, 5. F, 6. T, 7. D, 8. A, 9. C, 10. A

CHAPTER 6

Reformations in England

The Politics of Reform (16th Century)

You Should Know

- The English Reformation emerged from both native developments and the influence of the wider continental Reformation.

- King Henry VIII broke with Rome largely for pragmatic and political reasons, but also appointed reform-minded officials who facilitated England's embrace of Protestantism.

- Two factions emerged in Henry's court: conservatives who favored the ways of the old church and progressives who leaned toward Protestant beliefs.

- The English Reformation proceeded in ebb and flow fashion until it was finalized during the long reign of Elizabeth I, who established both a Protestant settlement in England and English power abroad through her skillful leadership over political and religious affairs.

- The reign of Elizabeth I firmly restored Protestantism to England via the Act of Supremacy (1559) and the Act of Uniformity (1559), the so-called Elizabethan settlement.

- The followers of John Wycliffe in England were known as Lollards.

- The Coverdale Bible was the first complete English translation of the Bible.

- By the end of her reign, Mary I was known as Bloody Mary.

- Spain was England's most powerful enemy during the reign of Elizabeth I.

Reflection Questions

1. Citing key persons and events, trace the rise of English Protestantism under Henry VIII.

2. Discuss the ways in which Archbishop Cranmer furthered the Reformation in England.

3. Was the English Reformation the result of developments in England or the continuation of the Reformation already taking place on the European continent? Explain.

Discussion Question

1. Identify and discuss the foreign and domestic factors that led to the English Reformation. In what ways were politics and theology intertwined in the English Reformation?

Quiz

1. (T/F) Henry VIII never wholeheartedly embraced Luther's ideas.

2. (T/F) The *Book of Common Prayer* was unabashedly Protestant from the start.

3. (T/F) Catholics became the objects of bloody persecution under Queen Mary I.

4. (T/F) The Elizabethan Settlement was essentially a return to Protestantism.

5. (T/F) Under Elizabeth I, England emerged as a major power on the European stage.

6. (T/F) Elizabeth I was known as the "Virgin Queen."

7. Which of the following was known as an ardent Catholic?
    a) Mary Tudor of England
    b) Mary Stuart of Scotland

   c) Reginald Pole
   d) All of the above

8. Puritans were opposed to:

   a) Clerical vestments
   b) The singing of Psalms
   c) Extemporaneous prayer in worship
   d) None of the above

9. The Act of Uniformity (1559) did which of the following?

   a) Proclaimed an end to hostilities between England and Ireland
   b) Re-established the use of the 1552 *Book of Common Prayer*
   c) Conferred the title of "Supreme Governor" of the Church of
      England on Elizabeth I
   d) None of the above

10. Which of the following strategies was employed by Elizabeth I's
Catholic enemies?

   a) Invasion
   b) Rebellion
   c) Assassination
   d) All of the above

CHAPTER 7

Refining the Reformation

Theological Currents in the Seventeenth Century

You Should Know

- The seventeenth century was characterized by an increasing concern to define, clarify, and defend the theology of the Reformers — a phenomenon known as "Protestant orthodoxy."

- Catholic orthodoxy defined the faith against Protestantism with a self-conscious embrace of Thomas Aquinas.

- Confessional entrenchment was not the only characteristic of seventeenth-century Protestant and Catholic theology, as both also witnessed a deep concern for piety and spiritual renewal manifest in groups such as the Puritans and German Pietists.

- The German Pietist movement grew within Lutheranism as a reaction against the perception of dead orthodoxy in the confessional Lutheran state church.

- Led by figures such as Philipp Jakob Spener and August Hermann Francke, and by institutions such as the University of Halle, Pietism emphasized regeneration, Scripture, sanctification, and church renewal. Protestant orthodoxy refers to a concern for correct theological content.

- Both German Pietism and the Dutch *Nadere Reformatie* were reform movements deeply indebted to English Puritanism.

- The Synod of Dort affirmed doctrines known as the "Five Points of Calvinism."

- The Rump Parliament: the assembly of English lawmakers remaining after "Pride's Purge"

Reflection Questions

1. Discuss the emergence, characteristics, and legacy of German Pietism.

2. Explain the similarities and differences between English and New England Puritanism.

3. In what ways does the theology promoted in the documents of the Westminster Assembly reflect the concerns of seventeenth-century Protestantism more broadly?

Discussion Question

1. Describe the major concerns and the development of Protestant and Catholic orthodoxy. Describe the Arminianism Controversy and what it teaches us about Protestant orthodoxy.

Quiz

1. (T/F) Jacobus Arminius denied the doctrine of original sin.

2. (T/F) The opponents of Cornelius Jansen accused him of being a secret Calvinist.

3. (T/F) German Pietism stressed a need for greater theological precision.

4. (T/F) English Puritanism was a diverse social and theological movement.

5. (T/F) James I of England was open to Presbyterian reform in the Church of England.

6. (T/F) Broad religious toleration was established under Cromwell's Protectorate.

7. "Hypothetical Universalism" or "Four-Point Calvinism" is a teaching associated with:

a) Amyraldism
b) Jansenism
c) Puritanism
d) All of the above

8. Which of the following groups is a legacy of German Pietism?

a) Moravians
b) Methodists
c) Holiness movement
d) All of the above

9. During the English Civil War Oliver Cromwell's New Model Army took up arms against:

a) The king's forces
b) Parliament
c) Scotland and Ireland
d) All of the above

10. Basic Puritan theology in both England and New England was set forth in the teachings of:

a) Anne Hutchinson
b) The Westminster Assembly
c) Archbishop Laud
d) John and Charles Wesley

CHAPTER 8

Christianity in an Age of Fear, Crisis, and Exploration (17th Century)

You Should Know

- Seventeenth-century Europe was a time of crisis, including staggering infant mortality rates, short life expectancies, massive death tolls from disease and famine, and the ravages of religious wars and political revolts.

- Art of the Baroque Period emphasized the emotional, turbulent, and grandiose.

- The seventeenth century was also an age of discovery, during which advances in science and culture and the exploration of the New World expanded knowledge of this world and the heavens around it and raised questions about ancient sources of authority.

- Religious divisions cut lines across the political map. Newly broken from Catholicism, Protestants turned against one another. These divisions contributed to anxieties about how a divided Christian Europe might fend off an impending Ottoman invasion.

- Although secular interests began to supersede religious commitment in foreign policy and the daily experience of Christians often deviated from basic Christian doctrine and ethics, the seventeenth century in Europe remained a culturally "Christian age."

- Amid manifold crises seventeenth-century Europeans sought comfort in both occult practices and the teaching and spiritual practices of the church. At the same time, ancient authorities were questioned in the face of new discoveries and cultural advances.

- Secular concerns began to take priority over religious commitments. All of these changes, however, took place within a European culture that remained firmly committed to its long Christian heritage.

- Clement VIII asked Robert Bellarmine to correct and revise the Vulgate Bible, the Latin translation of Scripture prepared by Jerome in the fourth century.

- Galileo advanced astronomy by making improvements to the telescope.

- Popular religion: a term used to refer to people's actual beliefs and practices

Reflection Questions

1. What motivated European exploration of the "New World"? What was the outcome?

2. How did the Catholic Church re-establish its strength and reputation in the 1600s?

3. What was the Thirty Years War about? Which groups benefited most from its resolution?

Discussion Question

1. Define the term "popular religion." Provide examples of this in the seventeenth century. Was the seventeenth century a "Christian age" in Europe? Why or why not?

Quiz

1. (T/F) Among the religious divisions of the seventeenth century was the animosity between the Jansenists and Jesuits within the Roman Catholic Church.

2. (T/F) The Lutheran Formula of Concord (1577–78) had an anti-Calvinist thrust.

3. (T/F) The *Magdeburg Centuries* was written to defend Roman Catholicism.

4. (T/F) The Dutch East India Company was a powerful force for Catholic missions.

5. (T/F) The Thirty Years War involved Catholics fighting against Catholics.

6. (T/F) Seventeenth-century European culture remained dominated by Christian values and symbols.

7. The exploration of the non-European world was motivated by:
   a) Piety
   b) Greed
   c) Power
   d) All of the above

8. King Henry IV of France had previously been a leader in which of the following groups?
   a) Lollards
   b) Huguenots
   c) Jesuits
   d) Uniate Church

9. Which of the following was NOT a Holy Roman Emperor?
   a) Clement VIII
   b) Ferdinand I
   c) Rudolf II
   d) Charles V

10. Some seventeenth-century Christians sought relief from the political upheaval and the devastation of war, famine, and disease through which of the following activities?
   a) Theological debates
   b) Exploration
   c) Fortunetelling
   d) None of the above

CHAPTER 9

Christianity and the Question of Authority (17th Century)

You Should Know

- The late sixteenth through eighteenth centuries witnessed debates over the question of authority, with "moderns" increasingly challenging the value of antiquity and advocating empirical and inductive, rather than "top-down," approaches to establishing truth.

- The impact of these debates over the question of authority was felt in politics, the church, science ("natural philosophy"), philosophy, and even in the domestic sphere of the home.

- Both Protestants and Catholics recognized Scripture's authority as the Word of God. But only Protestants affirmed Scripture's sufficiency for all matters of faith and practice pertaining to salvation. Catholics asserted that tradition reveals things not contained in Scripture and was a guide to the proper interpretation of Scripture.

- Although the question of authority brought change to many areas of seventeenth-century life through a new openness to challenging older structures and assumptions, the mindset and experience of most Europeans continued to reflect the traditions of Christianity.

- Tsars were Russian rulers who claimed absolute power in the seventeenth century.

- The combination of monarchy and democracy that developed in England near the end of the seventeenth century is known as constitutional monarchy.

- The category of probable certitude permitted scientists to move forward in their investigations based on premises for which they did not possess absolute proof.

Reflection Questions

1. Contrast seventeenth-century Catholic and Protestant perspectives on the authority and sufficiency of Scripture. What role did tradition, including creeds, play for either side?

2. Why was Galileo put on trial in 1633? Explain his view of the Bible and its authority.

3. How did the seventeenth century's questions of authority impact Europe's identity as a "Christian" and "top-down" society? Give specific examples to support your answer.

Discussion Question

1. What is a comprehensive "Christian worldview" and why did it become important to Christians in the seventeenth century to articulate such a perspective?

Quiz

1. (T/F) Most seventeenth-century European monarchs believed that their authority derived from the consent of the people.

2. (T/F) Absolute monarchy was difficult to implement in actual practice.

3. (T/F) Some people in the seventeenth century associated Calvinism with rebellion.

4. (T/F) Both Catholics and Protestants in the seventeenth century believed that Scripture's authority stems from the authority of its divine author.

5. (T/F) Protestants rejected the authority of creeds and confessional documents.

6. (T/F) Galileo denied the Bible's infallibility as God's revelation.

7. Protestants countered Catholic claims that the church is necessary to interpret the Bible with:

   a) The teaching that Scripture interprets Scripture
   b) The Bible is the final judge of creeds
   c) The Bible is the final judge of confessions
   d) All of the above

8. Some seventeenth-century Christians sought relief from the political upheaval and the devastation of, famine, and disease in:

   a) Theological debates
   b) Exploration
   c) Fortunetelling
   d) None of the above

9. The "Third Estate" refers to which of the following groups in seventeenth-century French society?

   a) Nobles
   b) Clergy
   c) Peasants and townspeople
   d) Monarchs

10. The category of _____ permitted scientists to move forward in their investigations based on premises for which they did not possess absolute proof.

   a) Probable certitude
   b) Probable possibility
   c) Probable uncertainty
   d) Probable impossibility

CHAPTER 10

Christianity under Duress

The Age of Lights (1680–1789)

You Should Know

- Despite the widely held belief that the European Enlightenment of the eighteenth century brought an almost overnight, comprehensive turn away from Christian faith toward the celebration of autonomous human reason, the actual shift in European culture was more gradual, less complete, and reflected a diverse range of "Enlightenment thinking."

- While precursors of Enlightenment thinking portrayed themselves as Christians, their writings were later used to support positions critical of traditional Christian teaching.

- Isaac Newton believed that natural philosophy (science) and biblical revelation did not contradict each other.

- John Locke's view of the mind as *tabula rasa* rejects the theory of innate ideas.

- Voltaire: a prolific writer, thinker, and social commentator deeply influenced by his experience of society and religious freedom in England

- Robespierre: a French revolutionary leader who carried out an oppressive Reign of Terror and justified this in the name of *philosophie* and reason

- "Age of Lights": the term *philosophes* used for the light of reason

Reflection Questions

1. How was the doctrine of Scripture's infallibility and authority challenged during the Enlightenment? How did Christians respond to these challenges to biblical authority?

2. Describe the contributions of Isaac Newton and John Locke. How did these thinkers relate their insights to Christian faith? In what ways did others use their ideas?

3. Discuss Enlightenment challenges to the traditional doctrine of original sin.

Discussion Question

1. How did the Enlightenment illustrate both reason's appeal and faith's persistence? Was the Age of Reason also an "Age of Atheism"? Why or why not?

Quiz

1. (T/F) The eighteenth-century Enlightenment was a decisive victory of reason over faith.

2. (T/F) Baron de Montesquieu attempted to discern laws governing human relations.

3. (T/F) French Enlightenment thinkers initially feared being jailed for their beliefs.

4. (T/F) The *philosophes* were masters of propaganda and self-promotion.

5. (T/F) Voltaire and Jean-Jacques Rousseau held similar views of human progress.

6. (T/F) Atheism was associated with social anarchy by some *philosophes*.

7. "Radical Enlightenment" is a term most closely associated with:

   a) Jansenism
   b) Anabaptism
   c) Atheism
   d) Voltaire

8. Which of the following is known as the "father of biblical criticism"?

   a) Isaac Newton
   b) Richard Simon
   c) John Locke
   d) Francis Bacon

9. Voltaire was a staunch advocate of:

   a) Christianity
   b) Social justice
   c) Republicanism
   d) None of the above

10. Diderot's goals for the *Encyclopédiae* included:

    a) Relating the various fields of knowledge to each other
    b) Revealing the general principles upon which human knowledge is based
    c) Changing the way people think
    d) All of the above

CHAPTER 11

Christianity in the Age of Lights (1)

The British Isles (1680–1789)

You Should Know

- British society in the eighteenth century was rapidly changing and socioeconomically diverse, as well as one in which Christianity made its enduring presence felt at all levels.

- In 1714 King George I acceded to the thrones of England and Scotland.

- Anglicanism began the century with the recent reestablishment of the Anglican Church during the Stuart Restoration and Glorious Revolution.

- Particular Baptists taught that Christ died only for the elect.

- Methodism began as a reform movement within the Anglican Church. Methodists focused on preaching, holy living, and a religion "of the heart." The powerful open-air preaching of John Wesley and George Whitefield brought many conversions among the poor and even within the aristocracy.

- John and Charles Wesley were deeply impressed with the piety of the Moravians that they met aboard a ship bound for Georgia.

- Roman Catholics did not enjoy full civil rights in eighteenth-century England and remained a very small minority of the population. Violence against Catholics was still an issue.

- Deism: a belief that claimed God exists but does not involve himself in his creation

Reflection Questions

1. In what ways did Anglican leaders seek to reform and stabilize the Church of England in the eighteenth century? Were they effective in achieving their goals? Why or why not?

2. Discuss the motivation, approach, and accomplishments of the "Evangelical Revival."

3. Explain the rise and decline of deism's appeal in eighteenth-century England.

Discussion Question

1. Describe the theology of John and Charles Wesley. What were their contributions to the church? Offer specific examples for each.

Quiz

1. (T/F) England refused to participate in the eighteenth-century African slave trade.

2. (T/F) Latitudinarianism sought to make Christianity more acceptable to intellectuals.

3. (T/F) The 1689 Act of Toleration granted Dissenters the same rights as Anglicans.

4. (T/F) The "Evangelical Revival" of the eighteenth century did not concern doctrine.

5. (T/F) The "religion of the mind" was a core emphasis of the Methodists.

6. (T/F) John Wesley believed that Christians could die to sin completely.

7. Anglican leaders in the eighteenth century were opposed to:
   a) Dissenters
   b) Roman Catholics

c) "Enthusiasts"
d) All of the above

8. The pejorative name "Dr. Squintum" was used by his detractors to describe:

   a) George Whitefield
   b) Charles Wesley
   c) John Tillotson
   d) John Bunyan

9. Which of the following individuals is best known for his arguments against deism?

   a) David Hume
   b) Joseph Butler
   c) Thomas Chubb
   d) Richard Baxter

10. Deism objected to traditional Christian teaching about:

   a) The resurrection of Jesus Christ
   b) Miracles
   c) Divine providence
   d) All of the above

CHAPTER 12

Christianity in the Age of Lights (2)

The Kingdom of France (1680–1789)

You Should Know

- The religious-political history of France during the Age of Lights was often dominated by the monarchy's struggle against two outside groups: Jansenists and Huguenots. During this period, France was both admired and feared as Europe's most populous and wealthiest country.

- France's absolute monarchy witnessed the erosion of its power in the Age of Lights as it battled challenges from both religious outsiders and a growing "court of public opinion."

- The various Christian churches in France weathered both the *philosophes*' intellectual attacks and the monarchy's attempts to control French religion during the Age of Lights.

- The spirit of Gallicanism was reflected in the willingness of French kings and bishops to defy the papacy.

- The Chinese Rites Controversy exemplified Jesuit missionaries' willingness to make major accommodations of Christianity to the beliefs of other religions.

- After a series of major defeats, the Huguenots became a suffering church, or church "under the Cross."

- "One king, one law, one religion": the dictum that governed French identity and royal policy during the reign of France's divine right monarchs

Reflection Questions

1. What was the significance of the Declaration of Gallican Liberties (1682)? Why did Louis XIV rescind it in 1693? What were its effects on French religion and politics?

2. Why was Jansenism viewed by some as a threat to the absolute authority of popes and kings? Do you think this fear was warranted? Support your answer with examples.

3. In what ways was the Age of Lights a triumph for Christianity in France? In what ways was it a defeat? Provide specific examples to support your answer.

Discussion Question

1. Compare and contrast the experiences of Jansenism, Protestantism, and Gallican Catholicism in France during the Age of Lights.

Quiz

1. (T/F) Louis XIV used religion as a means of supporting absolute monarchy.

2. (T/F) Critics of Jansenism accused its followers of being crypto-Protestants.

3. (T/F) Louis XV is known for his decisive action against religious minorities.

4. (T/F) *Unigenitus* was a papal bull that defended the doctrines of Jansenism.

5. (T/F) Jesuits supported the absolute authority of the pope.

6. (T/F) The Gallican Catholic Church had a dominant influence on the life of the French people during the Age of Lights.

7. The French monarchy in the Age of Lights felt threatened by:

    a) Augustinian Catholics
    b) Reformed Protestants
    c) Both A & B
    d) None of the above

8. Jansenists were critical of Molinism because its teachings:

    a) Originated in Spain
    b) Granted too much power to human ability in salvation
    c) Followed Augustine's teaching too closely
    d) Promoted papal monarchy

9. The idea that Christians can attain "pure love" was espoused by:

    a) Madame Guyon
    b) King Louis XIV
    c) Cardinal Mazarin
    d) Antoine Court

10. Antoine Court did which of the following?

    a) Provided leadership to the outlawed Protestant "Church of the Desert"
    b) Founded a clandestine seminary in Lausanne, Switzerland
    c) Urged fellow Protestants to submit to the monarchy except in matters of worship
    d) All of the above

ANSWER KEY

1. T, 2. T, 3. F, 4. F, 5. T, 6. T, 7. C, 8. B, 9. A, 10. D

CHAPTER 13

Christianity in the Age of Lights (3)

The Continent of Europe (1680–1789)

You Should Know

- Christianity persisted on the Continent during the Age of Lights, but its influence on culture was diminished despite the fact that most Europeans self-identified as "Christian."

- Various degrees of "Enlightened" approaches to government and religion emerged in different places alongside vocal opposition to such reforms.

- Eighteenth-century manifestations of religious life on the Continent were diverse from region to region and thus defy easy descriptions.

- The University of Halle was an important center of Pietist learning and missions.

- Neologians were German theologians who sought to accommodate Christian theology to reason and to new findings in science and biblical criticism.

- In 1766 a theater opened in Geneva, reversing the Consistory's ban on these.

- Phanariots were privileged Greeks who enjoyed the favor of Turkish sultans.

- Most Europeans in 1789 still considered themselves broadly "Christian," although the power of the Christian faith to influence culture and customs had certainly diminished.

- A sizeable minority emerged that had little or no involvement with the Christian churches.

Reflection Questions

1. Describe the development of Pietism in Brandenburg-Prussia and Moravia and discuss its influence beyond these areas. Cite specific examples to support your answer.

2. Compare different models of religious toleration in eighteenth-century Europe.

3. Describe the impact of developments during the Age of Lights on the Roman papacy.

Discussion Question

1. Providing specific examples, discuss the challenges to the Bible's authority that arose during the German Enlightenment as well as various responses to these challenges.

Quiz

1. (T/F) Germany in 1680–1789 was a single, unified state.

2. (T/F) Frederick the Great of Prussia promoted "enlightened" views in Germany.

3. (T/F) The University of Göttingen was founded to train pastors and missionaries.

4. (T/F) J. P. Gabler believed that the Bible contains "myths" from primitive cultures.

5. (T/F) Scandinavia was predominantly Roman Catholic in the eighteenth century.

6. (T/F) Spain in the eighteenth century took on elements of French culture.

7. Which of the following is associated with the principle, "the harder reading is better than the easy," when comparing biblical manuscripts?

a) Johann Albrecht Bengel
b) Jakob Spener
c) Pope Clement XI
d) Johann Philipp Gabler

8. Gottfried Ephraim Lessing argued that an "ugly, broad ditch" separated:

a) Eternal truth and historical realities
b) England and France
c) Scripture and science
d) Faith and reason

9. "Josephism" refers to:

a) A style of dancing that became popular in eighteenth-century Geneva
b) Mystical interpretation of the Old Testament
c) A program for reforming church and state in Austria
d) None of the above

10. Which of the following was NOT a ruler of Russia?

a) Peter the Great
b) Catherine the Great
c) James the Great
d) None of the above

ANSWER KEY
1. F, 2. T, 3. F, 4. T, 5. F, 6. T, 7. A, 8. A, 9. C, 10. C

CHAPTER 14

Christianity in an Age of Revolutions (1770–1848)

You Should Know

- The most prominent in what has been called the "Democratic Age of Revolutions," the French Revolution shocked, reviled, and inspired millions in Europe and the Americas with the rapid fall of France's "Old Regime" and the Gallican church that supported it.

- Various causes—religious, political, and economic—stood behind the revolts of 1770–1848, and equally diverse factors motivated anti-revolutionary and restoration partisans.

- While revolutionary proponents of liberal democratic republicanism often saw their cause as antithetical to Christian faith, and opponents of revolution often viewed themselves as defenders of the faith, others argued for the compatibility of Christianity and democracy.

- Although the Age of Revolutions ended with the apparent victory of restoration forces, Christianity no longer possessed its former ability to influence and form European culture.

- "The Age of Democratic Revolutions" was a period of upheaval across Europe and the Americas. Revolutionary and restoration forces alternately pressed their agendas. For most revolutionaries, their gospel of "republican democracy" was hostile to Christianity.

- Marx said that "religion is the opiate of the people," opening them to exploitation.

- Slavophiles: Russian nationalists who opposed "Westernization"
- Jacobins: the revolutionaries led by Robespierre

Reflection Questions

1. In what sense were Robespierre and the Jacobins, as they claimed, defenders of liberty and republicanism? How were they not? Support your answer with specific examples.

2. Describe responses to the French Revolution among European and American contemporaries. Why was it appealing to some, appalling to others?

3. Were the ideals that drove the French Revolution advanced under Napoleon Bonaparte? Why or why not?

Discussion Question

1. Discuss the attitude of various groups toward Christianity during the Age of Revolutions.

Quiz

1. (T/F) The origins of the French Revolution are clearly rooted in class struggle.

2. (T/F) Federalists of the Convention government believed that dictatorship was necessary for protecting the interests of the French Revolution.

3. (T/F) "The Civil Constitution of the Clergy" fueled counterrevolutionary sentiment.

4. (T/F) The Congress of Vienna resulted in the restoration of lands and thrones.

5. (T/F) Tsar Nicholas I of Russia helped suppress revolutionaries across Europe.

6. (T/F) Pope Pius IX was initially open to democratic republicanism in Italy.

7. Which of the following best describes how French revolutionaries defined "revolution"?

   a) The return to a previous form of existence
   b) The initiation of a new order
   c) The movement of the earth around the sun
   d) All of the above

8. Because the general public rejected the Cult of Reason, Robespierre established:

   a) The Gallican Catholic Church
   b) The Reign of Terror
   c) The Cult of the Supreme Being
   d) None of the above

9. Who criticized the French Revolution's basis in natural law?

   a) John Wesley
   b) Edmund Burke
   c) Pope Pius IX
   d) Thomas Jefferson

10. Which of the following frustrated efforts to form a politically liberal Germany in 1848–49?

   a) The restoration of conservative aristocrats to power in Berlin
   b) The Austrian emperor's decision to create an Austrian Hapsburg state
   c) Friedrick William IV's refusal of a crown from the German National Assembly
   d) All of the above

CHAPTER 15

Adjusting to Modernization and Secularism

The Rise of Protestant Liberalism (1799–1919)

You Should Know

- Christians struggled to relate traditional faith with modern developments, with some abandoning their faith, others reasserting the authority of traditional doctrine and the church, and still others searching for ways to reconcile faith and modern science.

- Protestant liberal theologians attempted to make Christianity appealing to unbelievers by reconceiving Christianity in a way that was impervious to empirical critique or by more enthusiastically embracing the methods and assumptions of modernity.

- European Protestant liberalism declined in the years leading up to the outbreak of World War I in 1914, which challenged liberal assumptions about human goodness and progress.

- The technological and mechanical innovations of the Industrial Revolution significantly increased Europe's economic and political power in the nineteenth century.

- Darwin proposed that the organic evolution of a species takes place by process of natural selection.

- "Modernization": the complex movement of a society from an agricultural, rural, and traditional condition to a situation that is more urban, industrial, technological, and generally democratic and pluralistic

- Friedrich Schleiermacher: regarded as the "father of modern theology" who argued that the essence of religion is a sense of absolute dependence on God, and that Christians should have faith like Christ, rather than faith in Christ

Reflection Questions

1. Are "modernization" and "secularization" different names for the same thing? Why or why not? Support your answer with examples from nineteenth-century Europe.

2. Discuss the impact and influence of Charles Darwin's *Origin of Species*.

3. What is "liberal Protestantism"? What forms did it take in nineteenth-century Europe?

Discussion Question

1. In what ways did traditional Christian faith come under new forms of attack in the nineteenth century? How did Christians respond? Summarize and describe those ways and responses.

Quiz

1. (T/F) Modernization is always accompanied by a turning away from religion.

2. (T/F) Nietzsche belittled Christianity as deceptive and "a religion of the weak."

3. (T/F) Charles Darwin's *Origin of Species* sold out its first printing in one day.

4. (T/F) Some critics of Darwin argued that his theories supported forms of racism.

5. (T/F) The philosopher Hegel had a profound impact on German biblical studies.

6. (T/F) A common feature of Protestant liberalism was a belief in Christ's divinity.

7. "Natural knowledge" was extolled by nineteenth-century thinkers for being:

    a) Rational
    b) Objective
    c) Scientific
    d) All of the above

8. Which of the following refers to applying scientific approaches to human breeding?

    a) Agnosticism
    b) Eugenics
    c) Sociology
    d) Vestigianism

9. Samuel Wilberforce argued that God was the author of:

    a) The Book of Nature
    b) The Book of Scripture
    c) Both A & B
    d) None of the above

10. Friedrich Schleiermacher believed that:

    a) The essence of piety is a rational account of faith
    b) Christianity is about having faith like Christ had
    c) Miracles happened as recorded in Scripture
    d) None of the above

ANSWER KEY
1. F, 2. T, 3. T, 4. T, 5. T, 6. F, 7. D, 8. B, 9. C, 10. B

CHAPTER 16

Nineteenth-Century Christianity in the British Isles

Renewal, Missions, and the Crisis of Faith

You Should Know

- The "long nineteenth century" in Britain, which included the long reign of Queen Victoria, was an era of tremendous political and economic growth for the expansive British Empire.

- The nineteenth century also witnessed large-scale missionary recruitment and activity from Britain to distant lands, including the interiors of the African and Asian continents.

- At the end of the nineteenth century, the Irish population was divided between those desiring "Home Rule" and others favoring continued union with England.

- Church attendance and the broad influence of Christianity began to wane after the 1880s.

- Romanticism: a movement deeply critical of what it perceived to be the excesses of Enlightenment rationalism, insisting on the limits of reason and the importance of feelings

- Romantic thinkers and artists such as Wordsworth and Coleridge could both support and hinder the Christian faith, affirming religious experience while rejecting traditional doctrines.

- William Carey: pioneered nineteenth-century British missionary efforts in India

- The Mines Act (1842): intended to stop the exploitation of women and children

- "Soup, Soap and Salvation": a slogan describing the ministry of the Salvation Army

Reflection Questions

1. Was the nineteenth century a high point in the history of Christian missions? Explain.

2. Describe the Victorian ideal of family life. In what ways does it reflect Christianity's influence on British society? Conversely, how does it obscure Christianity's impact?

3. Was there a "crisis of faith" in the Victorian Period? Explain.

Discussion Question

1. What distinguished different groups within nineteenth-century Anglicanism and what concerns did they hold in common? Give specific examples of key figures and ideas.

Quiz

1. (T/F) Building the British Empire was associated with altruistic and evangelistic motives.

2. (T/F) The Oxford Movement sought to reconcile Anglicanism with other religions.

3. (T/F) The situation of British Roman Catholics improved in the nineteenth century.

4. (T/F) The Free Church of Scotland was Scotland's largest denomination in the 1800s.

5. (T/F) The Welsh Revival of 1904–05 was one of several revivals taking place in different nations at the dawn of the twentieth century.

6. (T/F) The majority of nineteenth-century Irish were Protestants.

7. "Romanticism" was an intellectual and artistic movement that:

   a) Challenged the Enlightenment's confidence in reason
   b) Celebrated the achievements of the French Revolution
   c) Promoted poetry as the highest form of human communication
   d) None of the above

8. Which of the following was NOT a characteristic belief of evangelical Anglicans?

   a) Supremacy of Scripture
   b) Human sinfulness and corruption
   c) Inward and outward evidences of the Holy Spirit's work
   d) Baptismal regeneration

9. Which of the following is associated with the Protestant Christian missions?

   a) John Henry Newman
   b) Mary Slessor
   c) Charles Simeon
   d) Samuel Taylor Coleridge

10. Which of the following claimed that he had never been a Christian?

   a) John Wesley
   b) William Paley
   c) John Stuart Mill
   d) Thomas Huxley

CHAPTER 17

The Christian Churches on the European Continent (1814–1914)

You Should Know

- In the nineteenth century Roman Catholicism saw signs of revival even as the papacy battled challenges from modern scholarship, Catholic liberals, and movements to incorporate the Papal States into a new unified Italy.

- The Pope called Vatican Council I, which asserted that papal pronouncements made *ex cathedra* ("from the chair") are above error and beyond reform. Pius's successor, Leo XIII, held similar positions but expressed a more welcoming attitude toward modern scholarship.

- In Northern Europe, France, the Iberian Peninsula, and Central and Eastern Europe, all of the various forms of Christianity had to adjust to new political and social realities that defied turning back the clock to the "Old Order" that existed prior to the French Revolution.

- Hostile secular forces did not prevent the Christian churches from experiencing revivals and confessional renewal, and from engaging in missionary activity.

- Despite unique regional circumstances and challenges, nineteenth-century Europeans still tended to identify their respective countries as "Christian," even as these "Christian" nations prepared for and entered into conflict with one another in the First World War.

- The Wahhabi practiced a "puritan" form of Islam.

- Søren Kierkegaard: writer and thinker who influenced generations of thinkers by promoting a "religious existentialism" that prioritized personal discipleship and denied that beliefs could be demonstrated rationally

- Young Italy: a secret society devoted to establishing a new, united Italy

- *Kulturkampf*: Otto von Bismarck's campaign against Roman Catholicism in Germany

- Commune: the rebellion that took over Paris in 1871

Reflection Questions

1. How did the papacy shape, and how was it shaped by, its nineteenth-century context?

2. Explain the Ottoman Empire's decline in power and influence in the nineteenth century.

3. Can one speak of a "Christian Europe" on the eve of World War I? Why or why not?

Discussion Question

1. In what ways did Christianity on the European Continent experience renewal during the nineteenth century? What were some specific challenges facing the churches in this era?

Quiz

1. (T/F) Pope Pius IX was known for his openness to modern scholarship.

2. (T/F) Kierkegaard held that beliefs could be demonstrated rationally.

3. (T/F) The Dreyfus Affair in France reinvigorated calls for the separation of church and state.

4. (T/F) Portugal was regarded as one of the most Catholic countries of Western Europe in the nineteenth century.

5. (T/F) The writer Leo Tolstoy upheld traditional doctrines of the Christian faith.

6. (T/F) The creation of independent Greek, Bulgarian, and Romanian Orthodox Churches in the 1800s reduced the influence of the patriarchate of Constantinople.

7. The First Vatican Council:

   a) Called for the frequent calling of councils
   b) Asserted papal infallibility
   c) Asserted biblical inerrancy
   d) Established a unified Italy including the Papal States

8. Which of the following is associated with Dutch conservative Calvinists?

   a) Otto von Bismarck
   b) August Tholuck
   c) Abraham Kuyper
   d) Leo XIII

9. The Boxer Rebellion involved:

   a) Resentment over Western influence in China
   b) The slaughter of missionaries and Chinese Christians
   c) The defeat of rebels by Western military forces
   d) All of the above

10. The academic discipline devoted to representing the forms of life that existed in ancient Israel is known as:

   a) Biblical archaeology
   b) Higher criticism
   c) Eugenics
   d) Biblical studies

ANSWER KEY
1. F, 2. F, 3. T, 4. T, 5. F, 6. T, 7. B, 8. C, 9. D, 10. B

CHAPTER 18

Global Christianity
A Re-Centered Faith
(20th and 21st Centuries)

You Should Know

- Globalization in the twentieth century resulted in greater economic interdependence and new opportunities for cultural exchange, which also profoundly impacted religious expression and Christian missions.

- According to tradition, Christianity was first brought to India in the first century by the Apostle Thomas.

- Since the mid-1980s the center of gravity in global Christianity has shifted from the West to the "global South" (Africa, Latin America, and Asia) where most Christians now live.

- The explosive international growth of the Pentecostal-Charismatic movement over its three stages is remarkable given its fairly recent inception in the early twentieth century.

- Major changes accompanying the shifting of Christianity's center to the global South include the need to address new issues of theological, economic, and cultural diversity, as well as the sending of missionaries from the global South into North America.

- African and Latin American bishops of the global Anglican Church have been especially active in efforts to reassert historic doctrine and traditional values. This has included initiatives to establish mission works and new Anglican provinces in North America.

- The Coptic tradition: identifies the Gospel writer Mark as the first Christian missionary in North Africa

- Vatican II: council that shifted the Catholic Church toward a greater emphasis on social justice and lay leadership that had a significant influence in Latin America

Reflection Questions

1. How has Christianity both changed and remained the same as its center of gravity shifts toward the people and nations of the "global South"?

2. Explain Christianity's development as a global faith in the twentieth and twenty-first centuries. What factors helped facilitate the spread of Christianity?

3. Define and distinguish the three "waves" of the Pentecostal-Charismatic Movement. How would you describe the Pentecostal-Charismatic Movement as it exists today?

Discussion Question

1. Refute the following statement: "Christianity is in decline at the start of the twenty-first century." Use specific examples in your response.

Quiz

1. (T/F) Germany led European efforts to colonize and annex portions of Africa.

2. (T/F) St. Augustine belongs to the tradition of Christianity in Africa.

3. (T/F) Christianity in China has grown tremendously despite government repression.

4. (T/F) Latin American Christianity has traditionally been deeply Roman Catholic.

5. (T/F) The Pentecostal-Charismatic movement currently possesses nearly one billion adherents worldwide.

6. (T/F) Church attendance in Europe increased throughout the twentieth century.

7. What percentage of the world's population was Christian at the beginning of the twenty-first century?

    a) One-third
    b) Half
    c) Two-thirds
    d) Three-quarters

8. Which of the following has posed challenges to the growth of Christianity in India?

    a) Conflict between Catholics, Protestants, and Thomas Christians
    b) The caste system
    c) Hinduism and Islam
    d) All of the above

9. Which of the following is associated with the Pentecostal-Charismatic movement's "third wave"?

    a) John Wimber
    b) The Azusa Street Mission
    c) Charles Fox Parham
    d) None of the above

10. Which of the following represents a missionary initiative led by the global South?

    a) The Episcopal Church in the United States of America
    b) The Azusa Street Mission
    c) The Anglican Mission in the Americas
    d) Wycliffe Bible Translators

ANSWER KEY
1. F, 2. T, 3. T, 4. T, 5. T, 6. F, 7. A, 8. D, 9. B, 10. C

CHAPTER 19

Modern Theological Trajectories

Spiraling into the Third Millennium (20th and 21st Centuries)

You Should Know

- The twentieth and twenty-first centuries witnessed unprecedented human achievement and devastation, which has had a tremendous impact on the shape of Christian theology.

- The impact of the two world wars on theological reflection is best understood with reference to the theology of Karl Barth, whose God-centered theological outlook replaced the man-centered view of Protestant liberalism and came to be known as Neo-Orthodoxy.

- Although subsequent generations of theologians have had to grapple with Barth as a point of reference, modern theology has continued to develop, in relation to shifts in cultural context and philosophical thought, along lines that bear little resemblance to Barth.

- The conflict between Barth and Brunner centered on the topic of natural theology.

- Central to the teachings of process theology is the idea that God is always evolving.

- Neo-Orthodoxy: the God-centered theological outlook that replaced the human-centered theology of Protestant liberalism after WWI

- Karl Barth: theologian who rejected the human-centered perspective of Protestant liberal theology, promoting in its place a God-centered approach that came to be known as Neo-Orthodoxy

Reflection Questions

1. Explain Karl Barth's dissatisfaction with liberal theology and describe his alternative.

2. Discuss how Christian theologians since World War I have attempted to articulate a theology that is neither "liberal" nor "conservative." What motivated such efforts?

3. How have various theological perspectives since World War I related to the Bible as a source of authority? Explain how such diverse approaches came into being.

Discussion Question

1. In what ways has twentieth- and twenty-first-century Christianity theology been shaped by cultural context? Provide examples to support your answer. What unresolved questions face Christianity as it considers the future? What lessons might the Christian faith draw from the past as it looks forward?

Quiz

1. (T/F) Karl Barth embraced the doctrine of the Bible's inerrancy.

2. (T/F) Barth claimed to teach universalism with respect to salvation.

3. (T/F) Roman Catholics have widely and warmly embraced Barth's theology.

4. (T/F) Liberation theology presupposes that God sides with the poor and oppressed.

5. (T/F) Womanist theology rejects the Bible and its authority.

6. (T/F) Evangelical feminism has been divided over differing interpretations of Scripture.

7. Which of the following said, "one cannot speak of God simply by speaking of man in a loud voice"?
   a) Albert Einstein
   b) Karl Barth
   c) Adolf von Harnack
   d) Jürgen Moltmann

8. Barth's theology is characterized by its emphasis on:
   a) Christ
   b) Revelation
   c) The Church
   d) All of the above

9. Which of the following are associated with promoting "post-liberal" theology?
   a) Moltmann and Pannenberg
   b) Henry and Van Til
   c) Frei and Lindbeck
   d) Barth and Brunner

10. Karl Rahner is associated with the controversial teaching of:
    a) The New Atheism
    b) Water Buffalo Theology
    c) African Traditional Religions
    d) Anonymous Christianity

CHAPTER 20

Catholicism and Orthodoxy

Collision to Collegiality (20th and 21st Centuries)

You Should Know

- Although imperiled over centuries of tsarist oppression and Soviet control, the Russian Orthodox Church has emerged as the dominant presence in a global Eastern Orthodoxy that includes the recent establishment of several Orthodox jurisdictions in the West.

- The Second Vatican Council was a revolutionary moment for the Roman Catholic Church as it moved away from its previous posture of anti-modernist isolationism.

- Vatican II set the stage for Catholic ecumenical efforts, especially with Protestants and Orthodox Christians, in the twentieth and twenty-first centuries.

- The papacies of John Paul II, Benedict XVI, and Francis reflect both the ecumenical spirit of Vatican II and a commitment to traditional Catholic values.

- As the Catholic Church continues to struggle with a widespread clergy sexual abuse scandal, it also faces an uncertain future tied to the shift of Christianity to the global South.

- The election of John F. Kennedy as U.S. President was a significant event for the acceptance of Roman Catholics into mainstream America.

- The Russian Orthodox Church began to grow after years of decline when Soviet leader Mikhail Gorbachev promoted a new policy known as *Glasnost*.

- *Aggiornamento*: a word describing Pope John XXIII's goal to bring the Catholic Church up to date via the Second Vatican Council

- John Paul II: one of the most popular popes in history, known for his ecumenical spirit, commitment to political reform, and criticism of American culture

Reflection Questions

1. How did the Russian Church become the leading church in global Orthodox Christianity?

2. In what ways did the papacy's spiritual authority increase as its secular power declined?

3. Discuss the impact of Vatican II. How did it change the global Roman Catholic Church?

Discussion Question

1. How has the Catholic Church both adapted to culture and resisted it in recent decades? Provide examples from the papacies of John Paul II, Benedict XVI, and Francis. Discuss present and possible future challenges facing the Catholic Church. How has the church attempted to meet these challenges?

Quiz

1. (T/F) Today's Eastern Orthodoxy is dominated by the Russian Orthodox Church.

2. (T/F) The papacy's spiritual authority grew with a decline in its secular power.

3. (T/F) Vatican II expanded the voice of laity within the Roman Catholic Church.

4. (T/F) Vatican II affirmed the existence of truth in non-Catholic religions.

5. (T/F) Vatican II reversed the Roman Catholic position on celibate clergy.

6. (T/F) The Catholic Church in America is the nation's largest religious denomination.

7. Which North American evangelical parachurch ministry is associated with a migration of its members to Eastern Orthodoxy in the 1960s and 1970s?
    a) InterVarsity Christian Fellowship
    b) Campus Crusade for Christ
    c) Wycliffe Bible Translators
    d) None of the above

8. Which of the following is associated with the First Vatican Council (1869–70)?
    a) Thomism
    b) Ultramontanism
    c) Anti-Modernism
    d) All of the above

9. Which of the following was the initial impetus behind the formation of Evangelicals and Catholics Together in 1994?
    a) A common concern for moral decline in American culture
    b) A common response to religious persecution
    c) Agreement on the doctrine of justification alone
    d) All of the above

10. A controversy that threatens to define the papacy of Benedict XVI is:
    a) The sale of indulgences
    b) The priestly sexual abuse of minors
    c) The activity of Catholic dictators
    d) Ecumenical relations between Catholics and Muslims

CHAPTER 21

Contemporary American Evangelicalism

*Permutations and Progressions
(20th and 21st Centuries)*

You Should Know

- Four basic theological principles—biblicism, cruci-centrism, conversionism, and activism—were expressed in the twentieth and twenty-first centuries by Fundamentalism, Neo-Evangelicalism, Postmodern Evangelicalism, and Post-Evangelical Evangelicalism.

- American fundamentalism arose as a conservative response to modernist theology and defense of biblical authority, but eventually divided over issues such as dispensationalism, evolution, and the use of tobacco and alcohol.

- The Neo-Evangelical movement emerged from the theological descendants of fundamentalists who retained their belief in biblical inerrancy but were more willing to engage culture, situating themselves between fundamentalism and modernist liberalism.

- Postmodernism, with its rejection of a universal worldview, has had a profound impact on evangelical Christianity, influencing matters of political engagement, social justice, ecclesiology, mission, women in the church, denominationalism, and ethnic diversity.

- Scholars at Princeton Theological Seminary vigorously promoted the doctrine of biblical inerrancy during the nineteenth and early twentieth centuries.

- In 1910 theological conservatives in America published a series of booklets entitled *The Fundamentals* as a response to theological modernism.

- Charles Finney: evangelist who popularized a method for promoting revival known as the "anxious bench"

- Billy Graham: evangelist who was widely regarded as the public face of American evangelicalism

Reflection Questions

1. Explain the formation and disintegration of American fundamentalism in the early twentieth century. What were its central concerns? Who were its key proponents?

2. Describe the new evangelicalism of Harold John Ockenga, Carl F. H. Henry, and Billy Graham. To what was this movement responding and how did it respond?

3. How has postmodern thinking impacted evangelicalism? Has its influence been positive or negative? Supply examples to support your answer.

Discussion Question

1. What are the defining characteristics of American evangelicalism? How have these changed over time? How have they remained the same? Specifically discuss various ways in which American evangelicals have viewed the Bible.

Quiz

1. (T/F) American evangelicalism is one of the world's smallest Christian groups.

2. (T/F) Early American fundamentalists were a diverse group united primarily by the common enemy they identified as modernism.

3. (T/F) Fundamentalists divided over views on abstinence from tobacco and alcohol.

4. (T/F) William Jennings Bryan bolstered public opinion of fundamentalism during the Scopes Trial (1925).

5. (T/F) The doctrine of biblical inerrancy continues to divide American evangelicals.

6. (T/F) Post-evangelical Christians tend to join the Roman Catholic Church.

7. Which of the following is considered by many to be the foundational principle for American evangelicalism?
   a) The frequency of revivals
   b) The authority of Scripture
   c) Speaking in tongues
   d) Social activism

8. Which of the following is NOT associated with the emergence of Neo-Evangelicalism?
   a) H. L. Mencken
   b) Fuller Theological Seminary
   c) National Association of Evangelicals
   d) *Christianity Today* magazine

9. Which of the following is a conviction shared by postmodern evangelicals?
   a) The rejection of a universal worldview
   b) The affirmation of gay marriage
   c) Asian-Americans as a "model minority"
   d) The inerrancy of Scripture

10. Postmodernism has impacted evangelical perspectives on:
    a) Politics
    b) Gender
    c) The nature of the church's mission
    d) All of the above

ANSWER KEY

1. F, 2. T, 3. T, 4. F, 5. T, 6. F, 7. B, 8. A, 9. A, 10. D

CHAPTER 22

Christianity and Islam

The Challenge of the Future (21st Century)

You Should Know

- The rise of militant Islam is the most pressing challenge facing the Christian church as it looks toward the future.

- The attacks of September 11, 2001 and their aftermath reveal a conflict far deeper than a war on terrorism, namely the clash between Western and Islamic civilizations.

- Despite academic predictions that religion would eventually be absorbed by secularism, realities such as the September 11, 2001 terror attacks on the United States demonstrate the ongoing potency of religion.

- The long history of violent conflict between Christians and Muslims has been intensified in recent years owing to the Saudi promotion of Wahhabism, the Arab-Israeli Conflict, and the militant Muslim portrayal of the United States and the West as enemies of Islam.

- Although it is impossible to predict for certain, current patterns suggest that over 60% of the world's population will be Christian or Muslim in 2050, with ten of the world's twenty-five largest states possibly becoming the scene of serious interfaith conflict.

- Many in the Arab world view the U.S. war on terrorism as a war on Islam.

- The modern state of Saudi Arabia is largely responsible for the spread of militant and punitive Islam across the Muslim world.

- The creation of Israel in 1948 has resulted in a series of wars in the Middle East.
- The Ayatollah Khomeini in Iran called the United States the "Great Satan."

Reflection Questions

1. In what sense is the conflict between Islam and the West about more than theological or religious differences?

2. Explain the spread of militant Islam in the twentieth century and the implications of this for the world as a whole, as well as for Christianity in particular.

3. Describe and explain the attitude of militant Muslims toward the United States.

Discussion Question

1. Has religion become less important as secularism has spread in the twentieth and twenty-first centuries? Explain.

Quiz

1. (T/F) Religion is no longer a potent force in the twenty-first century.

2. (T/F) The conflict between Islam and the West can be explained by theological differences.

3. (T/F) Militant Islam has spread with the help of petroleum revenues.

4. (T/F) The Iranian Revolution of 1979 was a rejection of Western influence.

5. (T/F) Many Muslims view leaving Islam as political and cultural treason.

6. (T/F) The 10/40 window has been the focus of much Christian missionary activity.

7. Which of the following has emerged as an immediate challenge to Christian faith in the twenty-first century?

a) The Pentecostal-Charismatic Movement
b) Militant Islam
c) Global illiteracy
d) Urban development

8. Which of the following is the site of the longest war ever fought by the United States?

a) Iran
b) Mexico
c) Afghanistan
d) Vietnam

9. Which of the following nations currently has conditions ripe for large-scale religious violence between Christians and Muslims in the future?

a) France
b) Israel
c) Nigeria
d) Japan

10. Which of the following is NOT a branch of Islam?

a) Sunni
b) Shiite
c) Sufi
d) Socinian

Notes

www.ingramcontent.com/pod-product-compliance
Lightning Source LLC
Chambersburg PA
CBHW010920040426
42445CB00017B/1931